wild and beautiful
Wyoming

Featuring the photography of Fred Pflughoft

American & World Geographic Publishing

Yellowstone Lake, Yellowstone National Park, greets a stormy sunrise.

Photographs by David M. Morris appear on pages 29, 49, 99

Photographs by John L. Hinderman appear on pages 32 (top), 37, 46 (bottom), 101 (top), 111

Preceding page: Aspen shadows, Bridger-Teton National Forest.

ISBN: 1-56037-141-2
photography © 1999 Fred Pflughoft
© 1999 American & World Geographic Publishing
For more information on our books call or write: American & World Geographic Publishing,
P.O. Box 5630, Helena, Montana 59604, (406) 443-2842 or (800) 654-1105.

Printed in Singapore

Foreword

Wyoming, the Cowboy State—a place where the Wild West lives on and that icon of an era is still revered and idolized. A place that has more cows than people and more empty space than any other state except Arizona in the lower 48. A place everyone seems to travel through on the way to somewhere else, unless headed to Yellowstone National Park.

Here you may notice some peculiarities with road signs at the junctions of the few major highways crisscrossing the state. To the uninformed traveler, it would seem that all roads in Wyoming lead to Yellowstone, as every town vies for the summer tourist business that supports it for the long winters that hit this high and lonesome state. Often the signs lay claim to the shortest or best way to Yellowstone or most scenic way to see Yellowstone. Yes, Yellowstone is a major drawing card for the state's tourism industry, as well it should be. With its wondrous geological features and abundant wildlife, America's first national park should be on everyone's travel itinerary at least once in a lifetime.

It's summer! Columbine in the Wind River Range.

But Wyoming is more than Yellowstone National Park, and that is precisely what I wanted to capture in the images found in this book. Wyoming has always been my home away from home, and now after spending the last several years as a resident I have finally been able to fully comprehend the lure and essence of this grand state. The past two years have taken my family to every corner of the state and all points in between. We have hiked, skied, and camped in some of the most stunning country ever created and in the process have discovered that Wyoming's great diversity offers a surprise around every bend in the road or trail.

Most people, when they think of Wyoming, think of the Tetons, or Yellowstone, or even the Wind River Mountains of west central Wyoming: places that tower above the surrounding landscape and have unlimited recreational opportunities. But scattered throughout the state, between and around the dividing mountain ranges, are other unique places of equally superlative beauty. Some of them are deserts with active sand dunes as large as any in North America and bright red sedimentary rock formations that look as though they were transplanted from the American Southwest. Some are canyons almost as grand as the big daddy of them all. Some are eroded rock formations that remind many of medieval castles and some are streams, rivers, and lakes that support some of the finest trout fishing in the country. Still others are unfamiliar areas of high alpine grandeur and crystal clear lakes that are little visited and seldom seen. But from an automobile traveling at sixty-five miles per hour on a highway fifty miles away, those distant peaks appear as little more than bumps on the expansive landscape.

It is my hope that, as you view these images I have spent long hours driving and hiking for, and photographed with countless rolls of film, you will see Wyoming with a new perspective. That you will see the whole rather than only The Park. Of course the whole is never really complete in a book of this type, and I apologize if I missed one of your very special places. I probably was there, but the light is not always perfect for capturing one of those special moments of a special place.

Each and every image on the pages of this book brings back a memory, a time in space indelibly etched in my mind, and I hope at least one will bring back a memory for those of you who live in or have traveled to Wild and Beautiful Wyoming.

Happy trails,

Fred Pflughoft

Summertime reflection of Beartooth Butte of
the Beartooth Mountains in its namesake lake,
in Shoshone National Forest.

The schoolhouse in South Pass City State Historic Site no longer rings with the 3 Rs.

Facing page: Hoback River in the Gros Ventre Range.

Sinks Canyon State Park, near Lander.

Above: Adoptive favorite son
"Buffalo Bill," William F. Cody.

Left: Indian paintbrush,
Wyoming's state flower.

Autumn whispers over the Chapel of the Transfiguration in Grand Teton National Park.

Elk have long enjoyed the National Elk Refuge at Jackson.

Right: Indian legend said that a giant grizzly trying to reach people hiding atop Devils Tower scored its sides.

Below: Freight wagon rests on Fort Caspar Museum grounds near Casper.

In Yellowstone National Park: Hot springs and aptly named Firehole River.

Facing page: Keppler Cascades.

The Tetons from Snake River Overlook, Grand Teton National Park.

Written by the wind on
Killpecker Dune Field
near Rock Springs.

Buffalo Bill Reservoir near Cody is popular with watersports enthusiasts.

Right: Challenging the Grand Teton.

Above: One of the last summer days in the upper Green River Valley.

Right: Mallards fight the winter chill in Cheyenne.

Facing page: Lower Falls of the Yellowstone River, Yellowstone National Park.

One of Jackson's famous antler arches is ready for the holidays.

Spring dawn greets the Tetons, as seen from Schwabacher's Landing.

Above: Summer morning mist rises from Beartooth Lake.

Facing page: Pondering the path ahead in the Wind River Range's Indian Basin.

String Lake mirrors the Tetons.

Facing page: Old Faithful Inn's great hall is a feast of rustic fantastic splendor in Yellowstone National Park.

Breaking trail in the Bridger-Teton National Forest.

Still snowy in July, the stark East Temple and Temple peaks rise above Deep Lake in the southern Wind Rivers.

Left: Osprey on guard.

Below: Whitewater kayakers seek out western Wyoming's many rivers.

A bevy of remote beauties near Jackass Pass in the Wind Rivers: left to right,
Haystack Mountain, East Temple Peak, Temple Peak, Schiestler Peak.

Right: Early winter view of the Wyoming Range in Sublette County.

Below: Ancient petroglyph near Torrey Lake, outside Dubois.

Left: The last herd has been loaded for market from these chutes, now in Grand Teton National Park.

Below: Bull elk out for an early morning bugle.

Left: Legendary mountain man and guide Jim Bridger began building his trading post, now Fort Bridger State Historic Site, in 1838.

Below: Haying the "new-fangled way" in Sublette County.

Facing page: Looking across to "The Bottle" (left of center) from the summit ridge of Squaretop Mountain in the Wind Rivers.

Above: Outfitter Kim Bright sets a packsaddle.

Right: Can this badger in the Wyoming Range be looking for Mr. Toad?

Facing page: Arrowleaf balsamroot carpet above Red Canyon near Lander.

Snow lingers into June on the Breccia Cliffs above Brooks Lake, Shoshone National Forest.

Above: Well said, in Sublette County.

Facing page: Sunset glazes 865' tall Devils Tower.

Above: Old Faithful salutes its
namesake inn, Yellowstone National Park.

Left: Coyote on the prowl for a winter snack.

Facing page: Red Canyon near Lander.

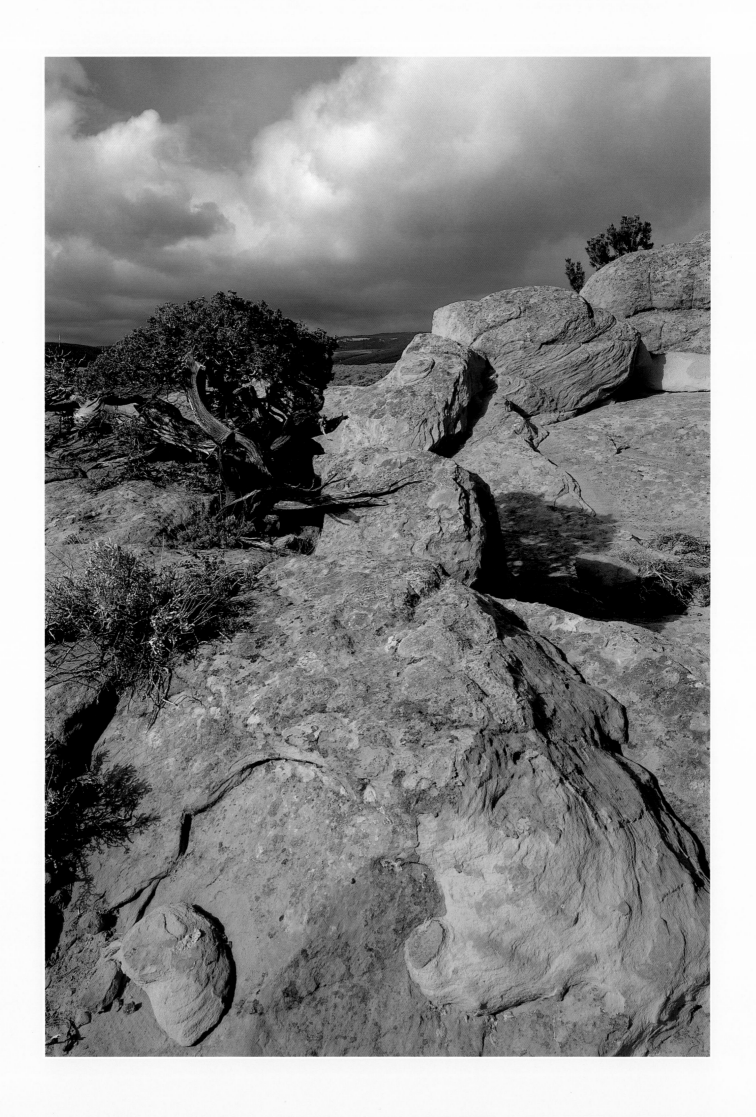

Roughing it in the Bridger Wilderness, Bridger-Teton National Forest.

Over the top at Yellowstone Falls, Yellowstone National Park.

Left and below at Fort Laramie National Historic Site: "Old Bedlam" bachelor officer quarters, dating from 1849, is the state's oldest military building; the stone guardhouse is seventeen years younger.

Cottonwoods, Wyoming's state tree, dressed in November frost.

Lower Yellowstone Falls, centerpiece of the Grand Canyon of the Yellowstone, Yellowstone National Park.

Good evening to the Tetons and Jackson Lake.

Eons of sandstone in Boysen State Park.

Medicine Bow Peak above Lake Marie in the Snowy Range.

Steamboat Mountain overlooks Great Divide Basin in Sweetwater County.

In the Wind Rivers, one of Fremont Peak's two glaciers challenges the August sun.

Facing page: Schussing the back country, Bridger-Teton National Forest.

Aspens give off autumn's golden glow in the Bridger-Teton National Forest.

Peaceful Island Lake in the Beartooths.

Above: Arrowleaf balsamroot busts out all over the high country during June.

Left: Lonesome Lake in Cirque of the Towers, Wind River Range.

As their living models sometimes do, cattle painted by local artist Pip Brant amble through downtown Pinedale.

Big Firehole Canyon, Flaming Gorge National Recreation Area.

Casting a fly, Mirror Lake in Medicine Bow National Forest.

Snow-coated trees atop Teton Pass, Targhee National Forest.

A climbing camp in the Wind Rivers' Titcomb Basin.

Facing page: Rappelling Vedauwoo Rocks near Laramie.

Above: Mark of the coyote on Killpecker Dunes.

Right: Flaming Gorge Reservoir, in its namesake national recreation area.

The lodgings atop Dinwoody Pass in the Wind Rivers may be spartan,
but the view of Wyoming's highest point—13,804' Gannett Peak—is incomparable.

Facing page: Hidden Falls trips through Cascade Canyon, Grand Teton National Park.

West Thumb Geyser Basin, Yellowstone National Park.

Right: Near Guernsey,
the Oregon Trail is a living presence.

Below: Summer is the time for many historical
reenactments, including the Platte Bridge
Encampment at Fort Caspar, seen here.

Point of Rocks Stage Station.

Facing page: Castle Geyser in Yellowstone National Park's Upper Geyser Basin.

Above: Back off for Beehive Geyser!
Yellowstone National Park.

Right: And they don't look right and left
before they cross the street. Near Farson.

Facing page: Looking down into
Cirque of the Towers, Wind River Range.

Badlands alpenglow near Marbleton.

A frosty sunset in the Bighorn Basin.

Just before the storm at Flaming Gorge Reservoir.

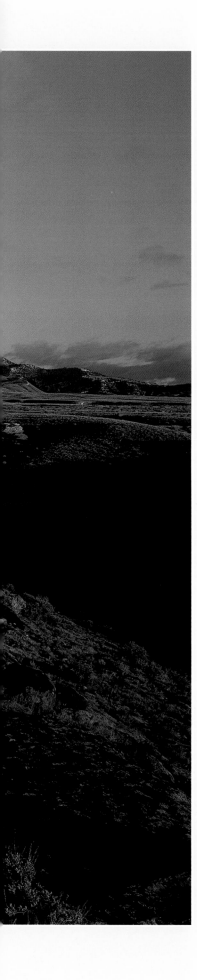

Above: Generations of horse lovers have walked through the door of this tack repair shop.

Left: Sunrise warms Heart Mountain near Cody.

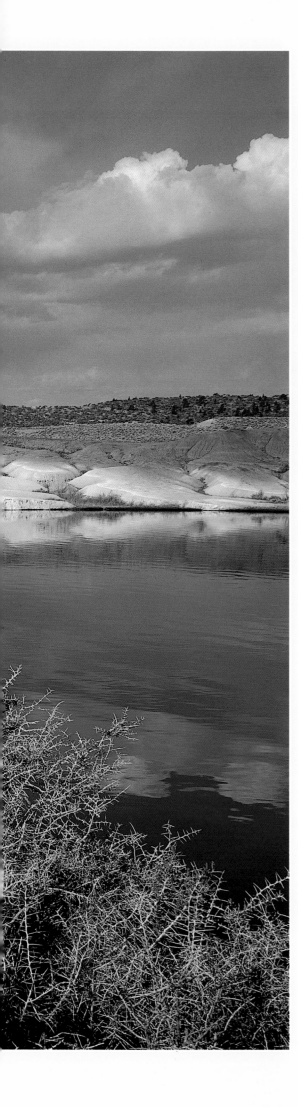

Above: December sparkles on Pine Canyon in Sweetwater County.

Left: Natrona County's Alcova Reservoir.

Looking past "The Patriarch" to the Tetons.

Day's last fire on Pinnacle Buttes in the Absaroka Mountains.

Squaretop Mountain and Green River Lakes, Bridger Wilderness.

Rainbow Terrace at Thermopolis Hot Springs, Hot Springs State Park.

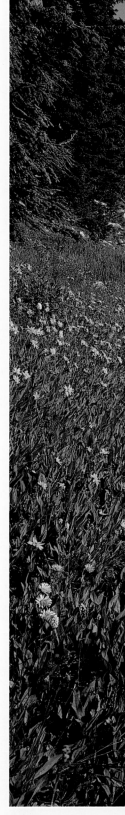

Above: Cooling off at Colter Bay Marina on Jackson Lake, Grand Teton National Park.

Right: Abundant wildflowers mark midsummer in the Snowy Range and Medicine Bow National Forest.

Sublette County cattle ranch.

Ten Sleep Canyon in the Bighorn Mountains, Bighorn National Forest. When crossing the Bighorn Basin, Indians expected to need ten days ("sleeps") to arrive near this halfway area.

The Equality State's gold-domed capitol rises above Cheyenne.

Facing page: Minerva Terrace in Yellowstone National Park was created by Mammoth Hot Springs.

Lupine beneath Cirque of the Towers, Popo Agie Wilderness Area.

Trumpeter swans forage the Yellowstone National Park's Madison River.

Above: American bison, nearly extinct in the early 1900s, are protected in Wyoming.

Right: Yellow-bellied marmot on the alert.

Facing page: An April day in Wind River Canyon.

A Cody landmark.

Plume Rock was an Oregon Trail marker for many a Conestoga wagon.

It just doesn't work as well if you use a four-wheeler.

The Owl Creek Mountains' rocky foothills rise abruptly from frozen Boysen Reservoir in Boysen State Park.

Oxbow Bend of the Snake River reflects Mount Moran, Grand Teton National Park.

Bringing in the winter feed in Sublette Country.

Above: Castle Gardens Scenic Area near Ten Sleep.

Left: The view from Montana to Wyoming across
Devil's Canyon, Bighorn Canyon National Recreation Area.

Storm heading for the Badlands near Dubois.

Bull moose looking for a party in Yellowstone National Park.

Out West at sundown.

Snowmelt spills out of Titcomb Basin in the Wind Rivers.

When they named Red Canyon near Lander, they weren't joking.

Arrowleaf balsamroot on the shores of Fremont Lake, Bridger-Teton National Forest.

Above: Visitors are taken back to the 1870s by the exhibits, demonstrations, events, and performances at Wyoming Territorial Park, Laramie.

Left: Wind River and the Badlands near Dubois.

High summer at Island Lake in the Wind Rivers.